10 - 20 - 30 minute card making

acknowledgements

10-20-30 Minute Card Making is the tenth in a series of books written by NanC and Company and published by Leisure Arts, Inc.

Author: Nancy M. Hill
Senior Design Director: Nancy M. Hill
Senior Editor: Kristine McKay
Coordinating Editor: Shannon Ogden
Graphic Designer: Rafael Nielson
Photographers: Shannon Ogden
                Rafael Nielson
Cover Design: Rafael Nielson
Copy Editors: Erin Madsen
                Vanessa Braswell
Card Designers: Shannon Ogden
                Erin Madsen
                Vanessa Braswell

For information about sales visit the Memories in the Making web site at www.leisurearts.com

letter from nancy

Dear Cardmaker,

There are few things more endearing than receiving a card with a special message in it. One of my most treasured keepsakes is a card that my father sent me while I was away at college. It was an Easter card (shown below) with a darling little bunny on the front with a tear drop falling from his eye. My father had such a delightful sense of humor and he lamented in the card that it was just as well that I was gone at Easter time because he didn't have to buy me an Easter dress! I have kept this card for more than 35 years because it is the only written message I have from my father and is such a reminder of his tenderness and great sense of humor.

The great cards showcased in this book allow you plenty of room to write your own message of endearment. Our staff at NanC and Company are excited to present the fun, quick and easy cardmaking ideas is this book. Our creative team, Erin, Rafael, Shannon, Vanessa & Kristine wish you success in "lifting" these designs and making them your own.

Happy Cardmaking,

Nancy

Nancy Hill

happy anniversary

step 1

Cut four 1 ½ inch squares* from coordinating pink and brown patterned paper. Lightly ink the edges and adhere to a 3 inch card.

step 2

Lightly sand the edges and the top of a 2 inch dark brown cardstock circle*. Attach alphabet stickers and adhere to the front of the card. Punch ten small holes along the edge of the card.

step 3

Thread ribbon through each hole and tie a knot.

* Templates can be found on pg. 56.

Tip: Do not be afraid to mix and match. Experiment by mixing multiple patterned papers together for a completely unique look. It is also fun to alter your text by using different fonts, colors, and sizes. Try cutting out various letters from word stickers to create your own distinctive message.

happy mother's day

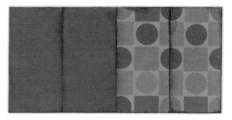

step 1

Adhere tan cardstock to the inside of a pink patterned 5½ inch square card. Fan fold into four even sections. Lightly ink the edges and folds on the pink patterned side. Punch two small holes on each end.

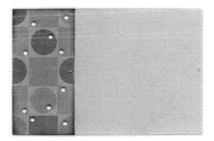

step 2

Randomly attach tan brads to the pink patterned side. Punch two small holes on each end.

step 3

Adhere tan cardstock behind an oval metallic bookplate. Spell "happy mother's day" with alphabet and word stickers. Tie a tan ribbon through the ends of the bookplate and the punched holes. Tie a bow.

Tip: Purchasing a printed card for your base is a great time saver. You can always bend it, fold it, punch out the middle, add something, or take something away to make it your own unique creation. The most important element of card making is simply "thinking outside of the box."

brothers

Tip: When matting photos, paper, or embellishments make sure that your edges are straight. The time it takes to get a "perfect" cut will pay off in the end with a cleaner, more professional look. Using a paper cutter instead of scissors is an effective way of achieving this result.

| step 1 | step 2 | step 3 |

Lightly sand the edges of a dark brown card.

Ink the edges of the circle paper and adhere to the front of the card. Apply a "brothers" rub-on to white cardstock, mat onto dark brown cardstock and adhere to the patterned paper.

Punch small holes on the top right side of the circle paper; thread three coordinating ribbons through, tie, and trim. Embellish with brads.

monogram

step 1

Begin with a 5 ½ inch square retro patterned card.

step 2

Adhere a textured cardstock monogram sticker to the front of the card.

step 3

Sand and ink a large square metallic frame and mount over the monogram sticker.

Tip: Sanding is a perfect technique for adding texture and softening edges. Textured cardstock with a white core will give you the best result. The grain of the sand paper and the motion that you use will create many different looks for your card. Remember sanding isn't for paper alone; try sanding on metal embellishments, photos, and stickers. A finer grain sandpaper will give you a subtle distressed look, while coarse sandpaper is great for doing a "cross-hatch" look on metals. To achieve the "cross hatch look" simply drag the coarse sandpaper across diagonally and then repeat in the opposite direction.

graduation

Tip: Vellum can be a fun element to add to your card. It can be attached with fasteners such as brads and eyelets. You can also use vellum tape or vellum adhesive spray. For a streak free result, place vellum face down inside of a cardboard box. Hold the can of vellum adhesive spray approximately 1½ feet away and lightly spray. Carefully pick up the vellum and wave it back and forth until it is slightly tacky. Once the vellum is dry attach it to your project. The vellum is repositionable for several hours after placement.

step 1

Lightly ink edges of a large piece of white cardstock and a 5 ½ inch square yellow card. Adhere the inked cardstock square to the front.

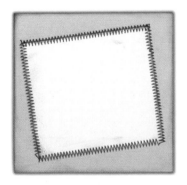

step 2

Zigzag stitch around the edges of the white cardstock.

step 3

Attach a vellum quote onto a piece of vertically striped red and yellow paper with vellum adhesive spray. Adhere to the front of the card and embellish with brads.

a friend

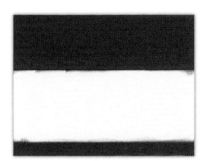 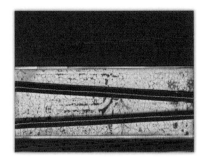 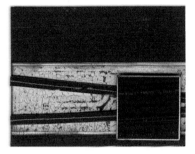

step 1

Lightly ink the edges on a strip of white cardstock and adhere to a dark brown card.

step 2

Mount a slightly smaller inked strip of "weathered" paper onto the white strip. Adhere two skinny strips of red cardstock to the front at a slight angle. Straight stitch down the middle of both strips.

step 3

Attach a clear "friend" sticker to a small piece of red cardstock. Mat with a piece of white cardstock, ink the edges, and attach to the card with pop·dots.

hi there friend

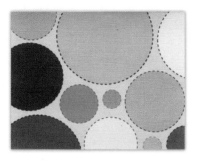

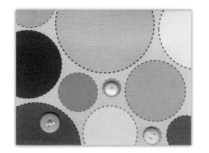

step 1

Begin with a circle patterned card.

step 2

Thread floss through three buttons and attach to the front of the card.

step 3

Use alphabet stickers to spell "hi there friend".

Tip: When using embellishments use odd numbers (3, 6, 9. etc.) Even numbers tend to cause a separation of the design while odd numbers create a visual triangle that pulls everything together.

thanks

Tip: Scraps are ideal for card making. Often the small paper scraps are perfect for matting photographs and word phrases. It saves time and money to organize scraps by color, in page protectors or folders, and put them in a binder or file box.

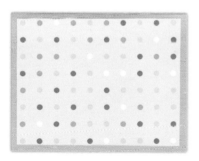

step 1

Mat pink and lime polka dot paper onto a lime green card.

step 2

Attach a wide strip of dark pink cardstock across the front. Zigzag stitch along the top and bottom with white thread.

step 3

Mount a piece of white cardstock behind an oval metallic bookplate. Spell "thanks" with random pink and green alphabet stickers. Anchor both ends of the bookplate with lime green ribbon and attach a dark pink brad through each end.

thinking of you

Tip: Make a list of birthdays, anniversaries, and other holidays throughout the year. Sit down once a month and make all your cards for the month. You may also choose to make the cards by occasions, creating all birthday or anniversary cards at one time. Use a file box to organize your cards by month or theme.

step 1

Tear the top and bottom edge of a multi-colored piece of patterned paper and adhere to the front of a yellow card. Lightly sand the top and edges.

step 2

Adhere a clear "thinking of you" sticker to purple paper. Trim and mat onto multi-colored paper. Attach to the front of the card.

step 3

Punch holes in top corner and tie ribbon through. Embellish with three green brads.

step 1

Double mat a piece of multi·colored paper onto orange and green cardstock and mount onto the front of a light blue 5 ½ inch square card. Lightly sand the top and edges.

step 2

Mount a piece of multi·colored paper behind a light blue 4 inch overlay so that a different color will show through each window. Attach a seashell sticker inside each window.

step 3

Attach blue cardstock to corners. Adhere blue gingham ribbon along the bottom. Place white cardstock behind a rectangle metallic bookplate and stamp the word "thanks". Attach the bookplate on top of the ribbon with two light blue brads.

Tip: Overlays can be used for much more than pictures. Some of the smaller overlays are perfect for cards. You can place patterned paper behind the overlay and alphabet charms or stickers in the windows. They work well for quick card making.

i love you

step 1

Begin with a pink 3 inch heart patterned card.

step 2

Use a rub•on to transfer the words "I", "love", and "you" onto coordinating cardstock. Double mat the words onto pink and red cardstock, tear around the edges and adhere to the front of the card.

step 3

Embellish the card with brads.

it's a girl

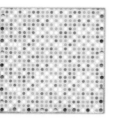

step 1

Attach pink polka dot paper to the front of a pink 5 ½ inch square card, lightly sand and ink the edges. Create a pocket by attaching pink brads through the bottom and sides leaving the top open.

step 2

Tear the right edge of a 4 inch piece of pink cardstock. Lightly sand, adhere to the front of the card, and attach a pre•made "shaker" embellishment.

step 3

Cut a tag out of pink cardstock and tear the bottom. Mount pink polka dot paper onto the tag and attach eyelets to the top. Lightly ink the edges of a piece of white cardstock and adhere to the tag, and embellish the top with brads. Use pink ink, rub•ons, alphabet stamps, and a thin black marker to complete the text.

Tip: Card swaps are a terrific way to increase your card collection and get new ideas. Make a card and duplicate it for each member of the group, then swap. It is fun to get together, share new techniques, and to build your own collection of creative cards.

little boy

step 1

Trim a piece of brown and blue striped paper slightly smaller than a light tan card. Carefully tear the top leaving it approximately 3 inches tall. Adhere a strip of coordinating polka dot paper behind the striped paper. Carefully tear the top and adhere to card.

step 2

Heavily ink the edges of the card and the top of a small piece of white cardstock. Attach the white inked cardstock to the inside of a brown cardstock slide and adhere to the front of the card.

step 3

Tie and knot white floss through a brown button. Attach the button and alphabet stickers to the slide.

Tip: If you are frustrated with getting a straight line when layering paper, simply tear the edges instead. Not only is it quick and easy, but it also gives a fantastic finish. You can achieve different results by tearing toward or away from yourself, by using a ruler and tearing the paper against the edge, or by using a quick ripping motion or slow short tears.

father

step 1

Lightly sand the top and edges of a retro patterned card.

step 2

Adhere dark brown cardstock inside of a blue cardstock slide. Lightly sand the top and edges of the slide.

step 3

Attach a "father" sticker across the front of the slide and fasten the ends with brads. Adhere the slide to the card at a slight angle with a pop·dot. Embellish with randomly attached brads.

Tip: Try not to "overdo" a card. Sometimes less is more, so keep it simple. Less layering saves time and creates a cleaner look. Remember when giving a card, it truly is the thought that counts.

welcome back

Tip: Inking is a simple technique to achieve an aged, weathered, and unique look. Simply slide the edge of the card along an ink pad, gently brush the card across the top, or ink the edges at a 45 degree angle. Ink can also transform the look of ribbon, photos, stickers, or embellishments.

step 1

Adhere two pieces of black cardstock to the top and bottom of a square black and white 5 ½ inch patterned card. Lightly ink the top and edges of the patterned card with black ink and the edges of the black cardstock with white ink.

step 2

Use metallic letters to spell out "welcome back", sand the edges, and randomly double mat some of the letters. Adhere the letters at different angles with some hanging off of the edge.

step 3

Embellish with green brads.

step 1

Lightly sand the edges of a navy blue card. Tear the top and bottom of a piece of green "friends" text paper and adhere to the front of the card. Lightly sand a small metallic bookplate. Mount to the card highlighting the desired word in the patterned text.

step 2

Attach three various shades of buttons to the top corner of the card with thread. Attach alphabet stickers to a small rectangle piece of navy blue cardstock. Mat with coordinating cardstock and adhere to the card. Sand the edges of a monogram alphabet sticker and mat onto a small piece of navy blue cardstock. Trim around the edges, tear the sides, and adhere to the card.

step 3

Use two strands of thread to anchor each side of the matted phrase. Attach green brads to the bookplate.

friends

Tip: It pays to make cards in duplicates. Often, the most time consuming part of card making is choosing the design, paper, or embellishments you are going to use. Once you have your supplies gathered, you might as well make several cards at a time. Give one away, save one for later, or put one in an idea box. It is amazing the great ideas you can recreate long after you have forgotten about a particular project.

we've moved

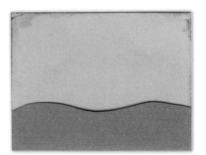

step 1

Lightly ink around the edges of a blue card. Cut a strip of green cardstock to fit across the bottom of the card leaving the top slightly curvy. Attach the bottom of the grass* with pop·dots.

step 2

Make thin cuts across the green cardstock without cutting all the way through to resemble grass. Cut out a house shape* with dark brown cardstock and adhere the heart to the front. Tie a white string around the house and adhere to the card. Adhere a 2 ½ inch red cardstock square with rounded corners* to the opposite side. Use pop·dots to attach the grass.

step 3

Round the corners of a 2 inch white cardstock square* and mount onto the red square on the front of the card. Handwrite your new address, decoratively outline the square, and add alphabet stickers to the bottom of the card.

* Templates can be found on pg. 56.

december 25

Tip: Ribbon is an inexpensive way to embellish cards. You can use ribbon for a quick border, wrap ribbon around the card, or use it to attach metallic charms or tags. You can also create unique designs by mixing and matching widths and patterns. For a masculine card, tie knots instead of bows.

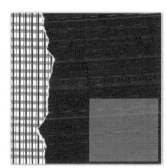

step 1

step 2

step 3

Tear the edge of a strip of red and green patterned paper and adhere to the left side of a red 5 ½ inch square gatefold card. Adhere a 2 ½ inch cardstock square to the bottom corner of the card.

Mount a slightly smaller piece of Christmas text paper onto the square. Lightly ink a skinny strip of white cardstock and adhere to the patterned paper along the left edge. Wrap adhesive ribbon around the card beginning and ending at the split in the front.

Trim around a desired word from the Christmas text paper and mat with white cardstock. Lightly ink the edges and adhere to the bottom left corner of the card. Attach a metallic bookplate to highlight the desired word on the text paper. Mat numeric stickers onto inked white cardstock and mount to the card with pop•dots. Embellish the card with brads. Wrap narrow ribbon around the card on top of the adhesive ribbon and tie a bow in the front.

wedding invitation

step 1

Punch out a 1 ½ inch square from the bottom right corner of a black 5 ½ inch square gatefold card. Adhere patterned paper inside of the card. Mount a transparent quote behind the punched out square.

step 2

Mat three coordinating 1 ½ inch squares* at different angles and adhere to the front of card. Adhere a ribbon around the card. Embellish with alphabet stickers.

step 3

Place a piece of cardstock behind a sanded metallic tag and handwrite the date. Thread the tag through one end of the ribbon and tie a knot.

* A template can be found on pg. 56.

Tip: Punches are great tools for card making. Various sizes of circles and squares are a scrapbooking staple. Not only do they give a more polished professional look, but they are also great for adding layers and depth.

wishing you'll feel better

step 1

step 2

step 3

step 1

Lightly ink the edges of a 5 ½ inch square floral card.

* A template can be found on pg. 56

step 2

Cut a 2 ½ x 1 ¾ inch piece of tan cardstock and double mat onto robin's egg and white cardstock, ink the edges, and adhere. Ink a 2 inch white cardstock circle* and attach to the center of the card with a pop•dot.

step 3

Punch three small holes along the top right edge and tie three robin's egg blue ribbons through the holes. Attach a circular "wishing you'll feel better soon" sticker to the white cardstock circle. Embellish the card with brads.

Tip: Card making doesn't have to be completely from scratch. Start with a patterned card and embellish with ribbon, stickers, rub•ons, and metallics, to make it your own unique design.

happy birthday

step 1

Cut two 5 inch circles out of retro floral patterned paper. Adhere cardstock to the backs and lightly ink. Set one circle aside.

step 2

To the other circle, apply a "birthday" rub·on to a piece of tan cardstock. Mat with coordinating cardstock, ink the edges, and adhere to the front of the card.

step 3

Attach alphabet stickers to small green cardstock squares to spell "happy". Mat with coordinating cardstock, ink, and adhere to the front of the card.

step 1

Adhere torn brown cardstock to the bottom half of the circle previously set aside. Apply adhesive ribbon.

step 2

Wrap narrow ribbon around the circle over the adhesive ribbon. Tie a bow at the top. Adhere patterned paper behind a vellum envelope. Cut off the flap and adhere to the card.

step 3

Adhere double matted stickers to the front of the envelope. Place both 5 inch circles together and punch three holes on the left edge. Thread ribbon through and tie three bows. Add a gift card.

Tip: Remember that a card can come in any shape or size. You can use CD cases, cardboard, coasters, paint chip cards, old mint tins, or anything else that sparks your imagination. It is a great way to create an original work of art.

best friends

step 1

Cut a pink card in half. Set one half aside. Tear the left edge of a piece of pink and brown patterned paper. Carefully adhere to the bottom and sides of the card to form a pocket, leaving the torn edge open. Lightly ink the edges.

step 2

Use brown thread to straight stitch along the top and bottom of the card. Adhere brown adhesive ribbon to the side of the pocket and zigzag stitch with brown thread.

step 3

Transfer a "friends" rub·on onto dark brown cardstock, mat onto pink cardstock, and fasten with brown brads. Spell "best" with alphabet stickers and attach to the card.

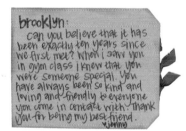

step 1

Cut a piece of dark brown cardstock into a tag shape*. Adhere a narrow torn strip of pink and brown patterned paper to the right edge.

step 2

Punch three holes along the left edge and attach three coral pink ribbons to the tag. Spell the names using alphabet stickers and embellish with three brads along the top .

step 3

Write a personal message on the other half of the pink card and attach to the back of the brown tag.

* A template can be found on pg. 55.

Tip: Pocket cards are a quick and easy way to customize any card. Use various sizes to create your own custom look. You can hand stitch or machine stitch the edges for added appeal. Try using transparency or vellum paper for the front of the pocket, so you can still see the contents inside.

50's party

step 1

Trim a piece of dark pink cardstock slightly smaller than a card. Cut a black and white border sticker to fit along the top and bottom. Sand and ink the edges. Attach black photo corners and adhere to the front of a black card.

step 2

Stamp the name across the front with black acrylic paint and stamp the date along the right edge.

step 3

Adhere black and white ribbon along the left edge. Paint and sand a small metallic tag. Attach white cardstock behind the tag. Create a flower using pink brads. Tie a piece of black and white ribbon through the top and attach to the card with a pop·up dot. Embellish with pink brads and black and white word stickers.

step 1	step 2	step 3

Inside the card, mat pink and black "funky" polka dot paper to the bottom .

Ink and sand dark pink cardstock and attach black photo corners. Embellish with random stickers, rubber stamps, and a trimmed self-adhesive border strip. Adhere the cardstock to the center of the polka dot paper.

Mat a lightly sanded dark pink cardstock strip to a slightly larger pink and black "funky" polka dot strip. Attach pink brads to the top corners and adhere the strip onto the top of the card. Embellish with rubber stamps, stickers, and handwriting.

Tip: Metallics can be altered in numerous ways to achieve a variety of unique styles. You can paint and sand the metal for a great "shabby chic" look. For a more polished appearance, spray on a layer of Gesso, let dry completely, and paint with an acrylic paint. Leave the metal with a matte finish or use a glossy spray for a shiny, eye•catching result.

hot summer days

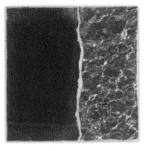

step 1

Cut a strip of water patterned paper, tear the edge, and adhere to the right side of a red 5 ½ inch card. Lightly sand the top and edges.

step 2

Attach a clear "hot summer days" sticker onto white cardstock. Double mat with yellow cardstock and bright polka dot paper, and lightly ink the edges. Wrap adhesive ribbon around each corner and adhere to the front of the card.

step 3

Embellish the card with brads and alphabet stickers.

step 1

Adhere torn water patterned paper to the edges of the card and lightly sand the top and edges.

step 2

Tear the edge of a yellow cardstock square and mount onto a torn inked polka dot paper. Punch three holes along the edge, tie ribbons through, and adhere to the card. Repeat these steps on the other side.

step 3

Embellish with stickers, hand-writing, and brads.

Tip: Adhesive ribbon is a hot new product that saves time and hassle. Simply peel off the backing and place in the desired spot. It is usually repositionable until you press and smooth firmly. For a unique touch, use it as cloth photo corners by simply tucking the ends around to the back.

what i like about u

step 1

Adhere a strip of green floral paper to the left edge of a green card. Apply adhesive ribbon to the seam.

step 2

Lightly ink the edges of the card. Zigzag stitch down the ribbon.

step 3

Apply a "what I like about" rub·on. Lightly sand a metallic "U", mount onto cardstock, and adhere to the card with a pop·dot.

step 1

Cut a piece of yellow cardstock 5 x 8 inches which is slightly smaller than the inside of the card. Attach brads along the left side of the cardstock and lightly ink the edges.

step 2

Apply a "2 peas in a pod" rub·on, attach a "cutie pie" metallic with brads, and handwrite a message.

step 3

Embellish the card with stickers, rub·ons, brads, metallic words, and handwriting. Adhere to the inside of the card.

Tip: Stitching by hand or with a sewing machine can be a great tool for creating an eye·catching card. To achieve a great decorative look, use a straight or zigzag stitch along borders, ribbon, or thin strips of paper. Add variety to your card by using different colors and thickness of thread.

just four u

step 1

Lightly ink the edges of a pre·made light blue tag card.

step 2

Spell "four" with lime green acrylic paint on purple cardstock. Trim into a tag and mount onto a slightly larger piece of blue and lime green floral printed paper. Attach a small square of purple and green striped paper with a large purple brad on the left side. Adhere to the front of the card.

step 3

Spell "just" on white cardstock with stickers and ink the edges. Double mat onto striped paper and light blue cardstock, and adhere. Mount polka dot paper behind a sanded metallic circle tag. Mat a purple circle onto a larger blue circle and adhere to the center of the tag. Attach a white "U" sticker. Place the tag to the edge of the card, thread a piece of ribbon through, and tie a bow.

Tear the top edge of a piece of blue and green striped paper and adhere to the inside of the card. Punch holes in the ends.

Adhere purple and green paper on to the center of the card. Glue coordinating buttons along the edges of the paper.

Embellish with alphabet and canvas stickers, vellum embellishments, and handwriting.

Tip: Avoid perfection. Sometimes little imperfections are what make a unique design. Don't be afraid to mix and match embellishments. Use random fonts and sizes to create a truly eclectic look.

'till i loved

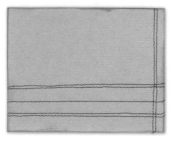

step 1

Use brown thread to stitch several rows along the bottom and left hand side of a pink card. Lightly ink the edges of the card.

step 2

Adhere a vellum, "'till I loved" quote to dark brown cardstock, lightly ink, and adhere to the card. Transfer a "love" rub·on onto dark brown cardstock, mat onto pink patterned paper, and adhere to the card. Attach brads along the bottom left edge of the vellum quote.

step 3

Transfer a flower rub·on to a small piece of brown cardstock and adhere to a sanded metallic bookplate. Vertically anchor the bookplate onto the right hand side of the card with dark brown ribbon.

step 1

Ink the edges of a piece of pink patterned paper and attach to the inside of the card.

step 2

Tear the right edge on a tan piece of cardstock and ink the edges. Mat onto sanded dark brown cardstock and adhere to the card.

step 3

Embellish with three coral red brads on the top right side of the brown cardstock. Create a flower with brads on the bottom left. Finish the card with a hand written message.

bridal shower

step 1

Punch out a circle from the bottom of a tall robin's egg gatefold card. Lightly ink the circle and attach to the top of the card with a pop·dot.

step 2

Attach a brad to a metallic alphabet charm and adhere to the inked circle. Punch multiple holes across the top flap.

step 3

Thread various ribbon through the holes and tie a knot.

step 1

Lightly ink a piece of robin's egg cardstock and adhere to the card.

step 2

Print the invitation onto yellow cardstock, ink the edges, and adhere to the card.

step 3

Tie pink ribbon around the card. Embellish with an envelope seal that can be seen through the hole in the front of the card.

Tip: Handmade invitations are the perfect touch for any event. The invitation is the first peek the guests will have. Why not make it an enjoyable one? It is a great way to show your guests how much you appreciate them and want them to attend. However, with all of the other party planning, don't let this be one more thing to add to the stress list. Why not have a few friends help? If it is a bridal shower, gather the bridesmaids together and have a card party!

a birthday wish

step 1

Mat purple cardstock onto a white card.

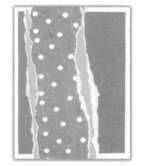

step 2

Tear a strip of pink and white polka dot paper and mount onto a slightly larger strip of torn robin's egg blue textured cardstock. Adhere to the card.

step 3

Punch three holes along the side of the card and tie robin's egg blue ribbon through. Embellish with white alphabet stickers, robin's egg blue brads, and an epoxy sticker.

step 1

Adhere a skinny strip of dark purple cardstock to the right edge. Adhere layered sheets of purple, pink, and robin's egg blue paper with the left edges torn, leaving the right edge short enough to see the edge of the purple strip. Tear the right edge of a robin's egg blue cardstock square, mat onto pink polka dot paper, and adhere to the inside of the card. Embellish with ribbon and brads.

step 2

Staple a premade pink and purple tag card together. Embellish with rub·ons, stickers, and handwriting. Use cardstock and numeric stickers to make tabs and adhere to the right side of the card.

step 3

Attach three small brads along the top right and along the left bottom edge. Embellish with random stickers, rub·ons, and handwriting.

Tip: A card is never just a card. A great thing about making your own cards is that you can personalize them. When giving a card to a friend, you could use their favorite colors or a monogram letter for their initial. Be sure to make the inside just as special as the outside. Do a top ten "what I like about you" list or add a special photo.

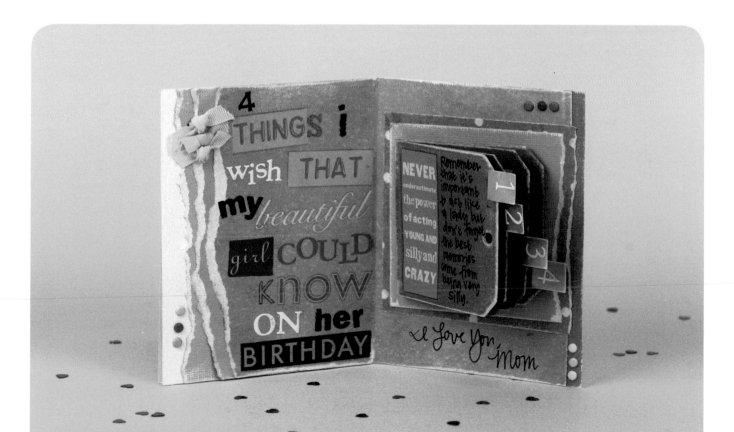

bundle of joy

step 1

Cut and adhere pink and green floral patterned paper to the front of a pink scalloped gatefold card.

step 2

Attach two eyelets to the top flap. Apply a clear sticker quote to a piece of pink cardstock. Double mat with white cardstock, lightly ink the edges, and adhere to the card.

step 3

Double mat alphabet stickers with pink and white cardstock and adhere to the card. Thread two different kinds of ribbon through the eyelets and tie a bow.

Amber Michelle Smoot

She came into our lives
on February 2, 2005
at 10:40 pm

Weight: 5 lbs 8 oz
Height: 18 inches

NEW
BUNDLE OF
JOY

step 1

Cut and adhere green cardstock to the inside of the card.

step 2

Print a message onto pink cardstock. Cut the top and bottom slightly smaller than the green cardstock and adhere. Attach a clear sticker to a piece of green cardstock. Double mat with coordinating cardstock and adhere to the card.

step 3

Mat a photo with white cardstock and pink and green floral patterned paper. Attach to the bottom of the card.

thinking of u

step 1

Brush the edges of a coral red and tan paint chip with ivory acrylic paint and sand the edges. Place the coral red paint chip on top of the tan paint chip, punch several holes through the top, and tie together with brown and coral ribbon.

step 2

Cut four 2 inch squares of coordinating patterned paper. Lightly brush the edges of the square with acrylic paint, sand, and randomly attach to the front of the card. Adhere a strip of coral striped paper at an angle across the front of the card. Place dark brown adhesive ribbon at the opposite angle right below.

step 3

Use brown thread to straight stitch along the bottom of the coral striped paper and zigzag stitch along the brown adhesive ribbon. Embellish with brown brads, white alphabet stickers, and metallic alphabet charms. Cut out the letter "U" from a brown cardstock 2 ½ inch circle*. Mount a coral polka dot paper underneath the circle and adhere to the bottom corner of the card with pop·dots.

step 1

Make an envelope out of dark brown cardstock*.

* Templates can be found on pg. 55 and 56.

step 2

Lightly sand the top and edges of the envelope. Tear the left edge of a 4 x 6 inch piece of coral cardstock, sand the edges, and adhere to the envelope at a slight angle.

step 3

Lightly ink the edges on a strip of floral patterned paper and adhere to the coral cardstock. Tear along the top edge of a painter's chip, and trim to fit on the corner of the coral cardstock. Tie three bows with coordinating ribbon and adhere to the card. Mount antique alphabet bubbles with pop·dots.

tall hearts

step 1

Cut out six tall hearts*, four from purple cardstock and two from light purple cardstock. Sand the tops and edges. Set aside three hearts.

* A template can be found on pg. 56.

step 2

Tear pieces of coordinating patterned paper and attach to the card. Adhere a 7 inch piece of wide ribbon to the back of the three hearts, space them approximately one inch apart. Attach two 13 inch pieces of narrow ribbon to each end of the hearts. Adhere the three remaining hearts to the back of each decorated heart so that the ribbon does not show.

step 3

Embellish the hearts with randomly adhered brads, matted cork alphabet stickers, handwriting, ribbons, metal flowers, and cardstock. Stack the hearts so the name is on the top and tie the ribbon ends together in a bow.

step 1

Adhere a 1½ inch corkboard square to the bottom right corner of a long vellum envelope.

step 2

Cut a 1 inch purple and green polka dot circle and adhere to the corkboard.

step 3

Lightly sand a metallic letter. Mat onto purple cardstock and adhere at an angle to the polka dot circle.

congratulations

step 1

Adhere two skinny strips of inked newspaper print paper to each end of a black gatefold card. Attach a skinny strip of inked black and white polka dot paper to the left edge and a thicker strip to the right edge. Attach three sanded black brads to the left side.

step 2

Embellish a small tag with inked "antique" text paper, stickers, brads, cardstock photo corners, and jute. Adhere the tag only to the left side of the gatefold card.

step 3

Use numeric stickers for the date and apply a page pebble to highlight. Place alphabet stickers onto black cardstock to spell the name, mount onto tan cardstock and adhere to the card. Attach lightly sanded black and white word stickers to the skinny polka dot strip.

step 1

Mat a piece of inked newspaper print and "antique" text paper to a piece of black and white polka dot paper. Adhere to the front of an inked white envelope.

step 2

Cut a 2 inch strip of black cardstock, attach three sanded black brads to the top and bottom and adhere to the card.

step 3

Attach a clear "Congratulations" sticker to a piece of "antique" text paper. Place a black sticker on top of the "C" for emphasis. Double mat with black and white cardstock, trim into a tag, and tie jute through a punched hole. Adhere the tag across the black strip. Embellish the envelope with sanded black and white text stickers.

30 minute card
••••••••••

christmas

step 1

Lightly sand the top and edges of a red scalloped gatefold card. Mat a piece of cork onto sanded green cardstock and adhere to the card.

step 2

Attach a large square "C" monogram sticker to a piece of red cardstock and lightly sand the top and edges. Embellish with three brads, double mat the "C" with "Christmas" text paper and white cardstock, and adhere to the cork.

step 3

Punch three holes along the left edge, thread red gingham ribbon though, tie, and trim. Mat square alphabet stickers with white cardstock and attach to the card. Adhere a strip of red gingham ribbon to the bottom of the card. Double mat a "December 25" sticker with white and red cardstock, lightly sand, and adhere to the ribbon. Embellish with a "Santa" sticker.

step 1

Lightly ink the edge on a piece of "Christmas" text paper, punch three holes on the top right edge and tie red gingham ribbon through. Adhere the text paper to the front of white envelope.

step 2

Attach a clear Christmas tree sticker to a piece of sanded red cardstock and mat onto green cardstock. Lightly ink the edges and adhere to the left side of the envelope. Mat a "party" sticker with green cardstock and attach.

step 3

Use alphabet stickers to spell the name on lightly inked white cardstock. Mat with cork paper, red and green polka dot paper, and red cardstock. Lightly sand the edges, attach three brads, and mount onto the envelope.

baby boy

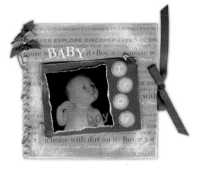

step 1

Cover two 5 ½ inch cardboard squares with light blue "boy" text paper. With the patterned paper on the outsides, hold together both squares, and punch several small holes down the left edge.

step 2

Bind card together by hand stitching through the holes with light blue jute. Attach a ribbon to the inside of both ends and tie a bow.

step 3

Sand the top and edges of the card. Tie three coordinating ribbons to the edge. Tear around a photo and mount onto sanded navy blue cardstock. Embellish with stickers, rub·ons, and small blue safety pins. Adhere the navy blue cardstock to card with pop·dots.

step 1

Create an envelope out of navy blue cardstock*.

* A template can be found on pg. 55.

step 2

Sand the top and edges of the envelope.

step 3

Apply a baby boy rub·on quote to a piece of dark blue sanded cardstock and mat onto a light blue "boy" text paper. Embellish the quote with tiny blue safety pins, and attach to the front of the envelope.

thank you cd case

step 1

Mat a 4 inch square of pink and orange horizontally striped paper to a piece of pink cardstock.

step 2

Adhere four sanded 1 ½ inch orange cardstock squares* to the front.

step 3

Punch three small holes on the bottom right and tie ribbons through. Handwrite a personal message.

step 1

Trim and lightly sand two pieces of orange cardstock to fit inside of a CD case. Adhere a piece of torn pink and orange striped paper to the edge of one of the orange pieces. Place inside the CD case on the right side.

* Templates can be found on pg. 55.

step 2

Attach a clear "thank you" sticker to a piece of horizontally striped pink and orange paper. Mat with pink cardstock. Place on a piece of vertically striped pink and orange paper and tear the top at an angle. Mat onto a piece of pink cardstock cut at an angle with the top torn. Embellish with brads. Turn the orange cardstock piece over and use the other side for the CD cover.

step 3

Tear the edge of a 4 x 4 ½ inch piece of pink cardstock and lightly sand the edges. Mount a 1 inch orange cardstock circle* to a 2 inch pink and orange striped circle*. Mount circles onto the pink cardstock. Tie a ribbon and mat the pink cardstock onto the piece of orange cardstock. Place inside the cover of the CD case.

Tawyna,
Thank you so much
for my birthday gift!
I love the earrings
and necklace! They
will be perfect for
Kara's wedding!
Thanks!
♥ Justin

Tawyna

birthday accordion

step 1

Trim an oversized piece of robin egg cardstock to 20 x 5 ¾ inches. Divide into 8 sections by folding in half three times and fan fold.

step 2

Punch out a 1 inch circle at the top of the first section. Mount a small piece of brown and blue polka dot paper to the back of the second section, so that the paper shows through the circle when folded down. Attach a numeric metallic tag with a brad. Punch two small holes along the edge of the first and second section and tie a bow. Handwrite "happy birthday" around the circle.

step 3

Adhere patterned paper to every other section. Have various people write a message on the solid sections and adhere their picture to the sections covered with patterned paper. Embellish with alphabet stickers.

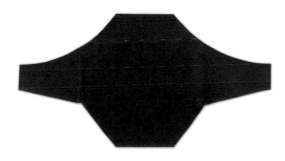

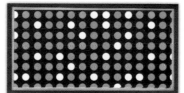

step 1

Make an envelope out of dark brown cardstock*.

* A template can be found on pg. 56.

step 2

Mat brown and blue polka dot paper onto light brown cardstock, ink, and adhere to the front of the envelope.

step 3

Stamp a name on dark brown cardstock with foam stamps and acrylic paint. Mat with tan cardstock, embellish the sides with brads, and mount to the front of the envelope.

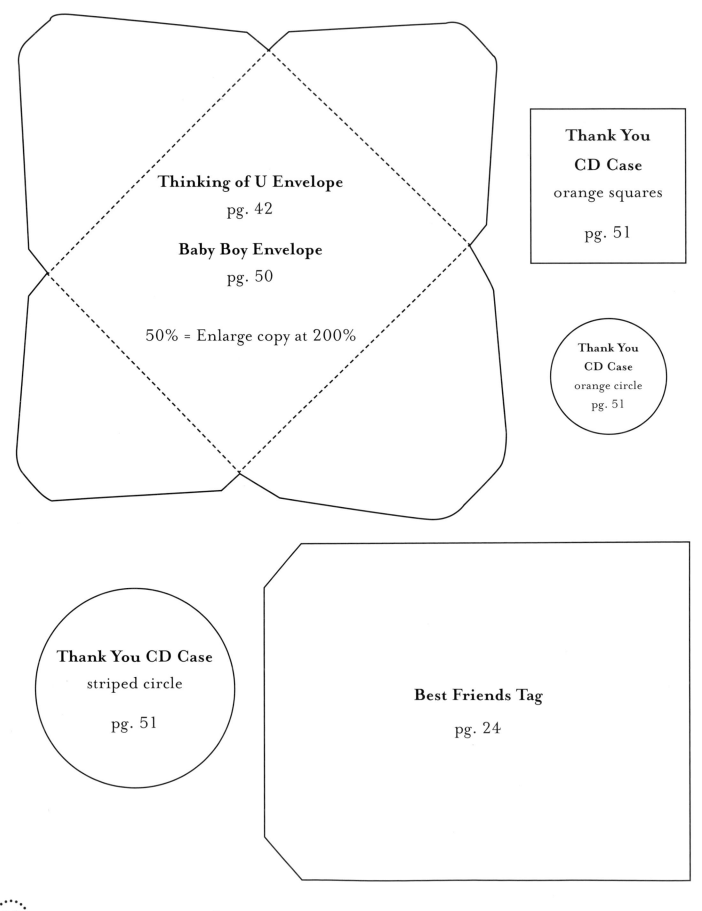

Thinking of U Envelope
pg. 42

Baby Boy Envelope
pg. 50

50% = Enlarge copy at 200%

Thank You
CD Case
orange squares

pg. 51

Thank You
CD Case
orange circle
pg. 51

Thank You CD Case
striped circle

pg. 51

Best Friends Tag

pg. 24

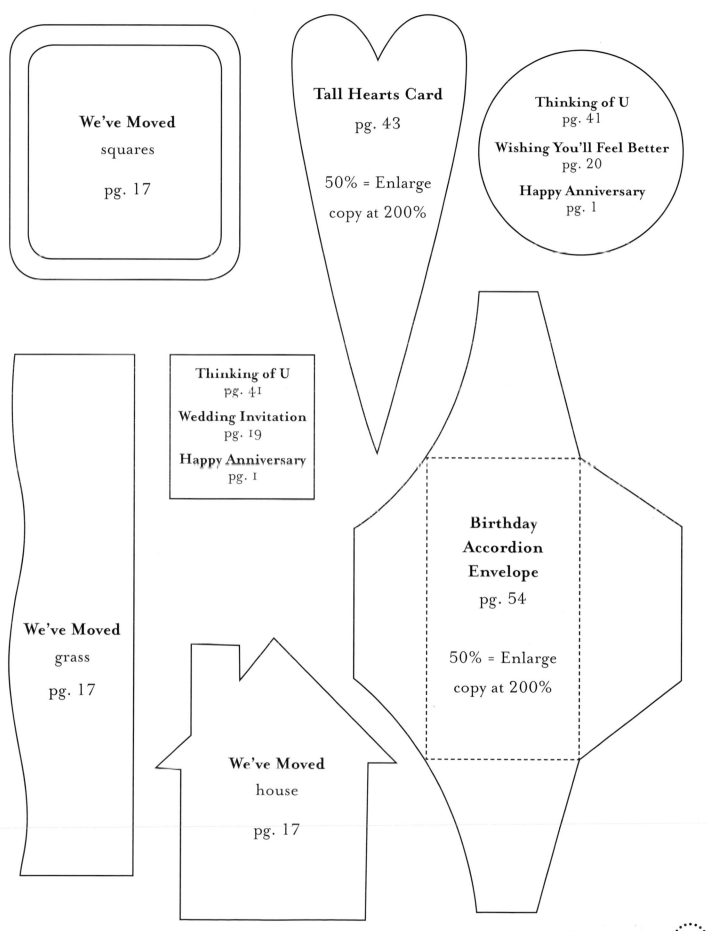

We've Moved

squares

pg. 17

Tall Hearts Card

pg. 43

50% = Enlarge

copy at 200%

Thinking of U
pg. 41

Wishing You'll Feel Better
pg. 20

Happy Anniversary
pg. 1

Thinking of U
pg. 41

Wedding Invitation
pg. 19

Happy Anniversary
pg. 1

**Birthday
Accordion
Envelope**

pg. 54

50% = Enlarge

copy at 200%

We've Moved

grass

pg. 17

We've Moved

house

pg. 17

10 minute cards

Happy Anniversary
Card: DCWV
Cardstock: DCWV
Patterned Paper: DCWV
Ribbon: DCWV
Alphabet Stickers: DCWV
Ink: Tsukineko

Mother's Day
Card: DCWV
Metallic Frame: DCWV
Ribbon: DCWV
Brads: DCWV
Alphabet Stickers: DCWV
Word Stickers: DCWV
Ink: Tsukineko

Brothers
Card: DCWV
Cardstock: DCWV
Ribbon: DCWV
Rub-On: DCWV
Brads: DCWV
Ink: Tsukineko

Monogram
Card: DCWV
Metallic Frame: DCWV
Monogram Sticker: DCWV
Ink: Tsukineko

Graduation
Card: DCWV
Cardstock: DCWV
Patterned Paper: DCWV
Vellum Quote: DCWV
Brads: DCWV
Ink: Tsukineko

A Friend
Card: DCWV
Cardstock: DCWV
Patterned Paper: Memories in
the Making
Floss: DMC

Hi There Friend
Card: DCWV
Buttons: DCWV
Alphabet Stickers: DCWV

Thanks
Card: DCWV
Cardstock: DCWV
Printed Paper: DCWV
Metallic Frame: DCWV
Ribbon: DCWV
Alphabet Stickers: Memories in
the Making
Brads: DCWV

Thinking of You
Card: DCWV
Printed Paper: Memories in the
Making
Clear Sticker Quote: DCWV
Ribbon: DCWV
Brads: DCWV

Seashell Thanks
Card: DCWV
Cardstock: DCWV
Printed Paper: Memories in the
Making
Overlay: DCWV
Ribbon: Offray
Alphabet Stamps: Hero Arts
Epoxy Stickers: Me and My Big
Ideas
Brads: DCWV
Ink: Tsukineko

I Love You
Card: DCWV
Cardstock: DCWV
Rub-Ons: DCWV
Brads: DCWV

It's A Girl
Card: DCWV
Cardstock: DCWV
Printed Paper: DCWV
Confetti Window Frame:

Memories in the Making
Brads: DCWV
Eyelets: JoAnn Essentials
Alphabet Stamps: Making
Memories

Little Boy
Card: DCWV
Cardstock: DCWV
Patterned Paper: DCWV
Slide Frame: DCWV
Button: JoAnn Essentials
Alphabet Stickers: DCWV
Ink: Tsukineko

Father
Card: DCWV
Cardstock: DCWV
Slide Frame: DCWV
Brads: DCWV
Sticker: DCWV
Ink: Tsukineko

Welcome Back
Card: DCWV
Cardstock: DCWV
Metallic Letters: DCWV
Brads: DCWV
Ink: Tsukineko

Friends
Card: DCWV
Cardstock: DCWV
Patterned Paper: DCWV
Metallic Frame: DCWV
Brads: DCWV
Buttons: DCWV
Alphabet Stickers: DCWV
Floss: DMC

We've Moved
Cardstock: DCWV
Alphabet Stickers: DCWV
Floss: DMC
Ink: Tsukineko

December 25
Card: DCWV
Cardstock: DCWV

Patterned Paper: DCWV
Metallic Bookplate: DCWV
Ribbon: DCWV
Brads: DCWV
Alphabet & Number Stickers:
DCWV
Word Stickers: DCWV

Wedding Invitation
Card: DCWV
Cardstock: DCWV
Patterned Paper: Memories in
the Making, DCWV
Metallic Tag: DCWV
Transparent Quote: DCWV
Ribbon: DCWV

Wishing You'll Feel Better
Card: DCWV
Cardstock: DCWV
Ribbon: DCWV
Brads: DCWV
Sticker: DCWV
Ink: Tsukineko

20 minute cards

Happy Birthday
Cardstock: DCWV
Patterned Paper: DCWV
Ribbon: DCWV
Rub-Ons: DCWV
Alphabet Stickers: DCWV
Pocket Envelope: JoAnn
Essentials
Ink: Tsukineko

Best Friends
Card: DCWV
Cardstock: DCWV
Patterned Paper: DCWV
Ribbon: DCWV

Rub-Ons: DCWV
Brads: DCWV
Alphabet Stickers: DCWV

50's Party
Card: DCWV
Cardstock: DCWV
Patterned Paper: Memories in
the Making
Metallic Tag: DCWV
Ribbon: Making Memories
Alphabet Stickers: Memories in
the Making, DCWV
Alphabet Stamps: Hero Arts,
Making Memories
Word Stickers: DCWV
Brads: DCWV
Date Stamp: Making Memories
Photo Corners: 3M
Paint: Delta

Hot Summer Days
Card: DCWV
Cardstock: DCWV
Patterned Paper: DCWV
Ribbon: DCWV
Quote Sticker: DCWV
Brads: DCWV
Alphabet Stickers: DCWV

What I Like About U
Card: DCWV
Cardstock: DCWV
Patterned Paper: DCWV
Metallic Letter: DCWV
Metallic Words: DCWV
Ribbon: DCWV
Rub-Ons: DCWV
Brads: DCWV
Ink: Tsukineko

Just Four You
Card: Memories in the Making
Cardstock: DCWV
Patterned Paper: DCWV
Metallic Tag: DCWV
Ribbon: Offray

Alphabet Stickers: Memories in
the Making, DCWV
Alphabet Stamps: Making
Memories
Word Stickers: JoAnn Essentials
Canvas Stickers: My Minds Eye
Buttons: DCWV
Brad: JoAnn Essentials
Ink: Tsukineko
Paint: Making Memories

'Till I Loved
Card: DCWV
Cardstock: DCWV
Patterned Paper: DCWV
Metallic Tag: DCWV
Vellum Quote: JoAnn Essentials
Rub-Ons: DCWV
Brads: JoAnn Essentials, DCWV
Ink: Tsukineko

Bridal Shower
Card: DCWV
Cardstock: DCWV
Metallic Letter: DCWV
Ribbon: DCWV
Brad: DCWV
Sticker: DCWV
Ink: Tsukineko

A Birthday Wish
Card: DCWV
Cardstock: DCWV
Patterned Paper: Memories in
the Making
Ribbon: DCWV
Alphabet Stickers: Memories in
the Making, DCWV
Rub-ons: DCWV
Epoxy Sticker: K&Company
Brads: DCWV
Mini Album: Memories in the
Making

Bundle of Joy
Card: DCWV
Cardstock: DCWV
Patterned Paper: DCWV
Clear Sticker Quote: DCWV
Ribbon: Offray, DCWV
Eyelets: JoAnn Essentials
Alphabet Stickers: DCWV
Ink: Tsukineko

30 minute cards

Thinking of U
Cardstock: DCWV
Patterned Paper: DCWV
Ribbon: DCWV
Alphabet Bubbles: JoAnn
Essentials
Alphabet Stickers: DCWV
Ink: Tsukineko
Paint Swatches: Behr

Tall Hearts
Cardstock: DCWV
Patterned Paper: DCWV
Metallic Embellishment:
Memories in the Making
Metallic Letter: DCWV
Rub-On Quote: DCWV
Ribbon: DCWV
Alphabet Rub-Ons: Making
Memories
Brads: DCWV
Cork Stickers: Creative
Imaginations

Congratulation
Card: DCWV
Cardstock: DCWV
Patterned Paper: Memories in
the Making, DCWV
Page Pebble: JoAnn Essentials
Alphabet Stickers: DCWV
Brads: JoAnn Essentials, DCWV
Jute

Christmas
Card: DCWV
Cardstock: DCWV
Patterned Paper: DCWV
Ribbon: Offray
Word Stickers: DCWV
Alphabet Stickers: DCWV
Stickers: DCWV
Brads: DCWV
Ink: Tsukineko
Cork

Baby Boy
Cardstock: DCWV
Patterned Paper: DCWV
Ribbon: DCWV
Rub-On Quote: DCWV
Alphabet Stickers: DCWV
Mini Safety Pins: Making
Memories
Cardboard

Thank You CD Case
Cardstock: DCWV
Patterned Paper: DCWV
Clear Sticker Quote: DCWV
Ribbon: DCWV
Brads: DCWV
Alphabet Stickers: DCWV
CD Case

Birthday Accordion
Cardstock: DCWV
Patterned Paper: DCWV
Metallic Number: DCWV
Ribbon: DCWV
Rub-Ons: DCWV
Brads: DCWV
Alphabet Stickers: DCWV
Alphabet Stamps: Making
Memories
Paint: Making Memories
Ink: Tsukineko

Look for these other Leisure Arts books

It's All In
Your Imagination

It's All About Baby

It's All About School

It's All About
Technique

It's All About
Cards and Tags

It's All About
Mini Albums

It's All About
Travel and Vacation

It's All About
Pets and Animals

10-20-30 Minute
Scrapbook Pages

Sources

3M Stationary
(800) 364-3577
3m.com

Creative Imaginations
(800) 942-6487
Cigift.com

DCWV
(801) 224-6766
Diecutswithaview.com

DMC
(973) 589-9890
Dmc-usa.com

Fiskars, Inc.
(715) 842-2091
Fiskars.com

Herma Fix
Herma.co.uk.com

Hero Arts Rubber
Stamps, Inc.
(800) 822-4376
Heroarts.com

JoAnn Essentials
Joann.com

K&Company
(888) 244-2083
Kandcompany.com

Memories in the Making-
Leisure Arts
(800) 643-8030
Leisurearts.com

Making Memories
(800) 286-5263
Makingmemories.com

Me & My Big Ideas
(949) 583-2065
Meandmybigideas.com

My Minds Eye
(800) 665-5116
Frame-ups.com/mme/

Offray & Son, Inc.
Offray.com

Pixie Press
(702) 646-1156
Pixiepress.com

Tsukineko
(800) 769-6633
tsukineko.com